HOW LOST IS LOST?

HOW LOST IS LOST?

Logbook of wacky aviation humor

Core F. Keller

iUniverse, Inc.
New York Lincoln Shanghai

HOW LOST IS LOST?
Logbook of wacky aviation humor

iUniverse, Inc.

For information address:
iUniverse, Inc.
2021 Pine Lake Road, Suite 100
Lincoln, NE 68512
www.iuniverse.com

ISBN: 0-595-30586-5

Printed in the United States of America

This book is dedicated to Josh Krecklow, Janis Smith, and my mother and father for their support and friendship and wisdom.

FOREWORD

"There's always time for laughter."—Core F. Keller

TABLE OF CONTENTS

JOKE LOG BOOK

Use the space below and create a log of the pages you like. Then, share this book with a friend or co-worker or aviation enthusiast!

Logbook:

Page: Comments:
Page: Comments:
Page: Comments:
Page: Comments:
Page: Comments:
Page: Comments:
Page: Comments:
Page: Comments:
Page: Comments:
Page: Comments:
Page: Comments:
Page: Comments:
Page: Comments:
Page: Comments:
Page: Comments:
Page: Comments:
Page: Comments:
Page: Comments:

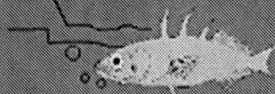

THE LIFE OF A PILOT

A pilot's life can be pretty grueling in case you were wondering. There can be a lot of waiting—for the weather to behave, for a clear runway, for the aircraft to be oiled and refueled—interspersed with brief moments of intense concentration and gut wrenching excitement and unfathomable frustration. But then there's moments of pure flying enjoyment that keeps pilots wanting to fly.

Most pilots spend a lot of time away from family and friends while traveling the airways keeping erratic eating and sleeping schedules and working under the constant threat of terrorism.

For the most part, pilots are those that seek a challenge, want to conquer fears, and take pride in doing things with precision.

FUTURE OF PILOTS

"Pilots don't have to worry about robots or computers replacing them at all. Passengers will never have complete trust with computers because machines do fail. But most importantly, pilots make great targets when things go wrong.

The small percentage of passengers who decide to test robot-controlled aircraft in the future will discount the risk especially if the airlines offer them incentive plans like direct routes with no stopovers and sobriety in the cockpit.

Pilots will take over the yoke now and then just to make sure the computer chips aren't overheating, exception errors aren't appearing in the tiny LCD screen, and that the in-board computer game isn't confusing the auto-pilot.

Pilots will also monitor things in case there's a computer glitch such as when emails do not reach air traffic control or there's program looping where the plane keeps landing over and over again in the same parking lot.

But airlines will begin using vending machines to replace stewardesses. For a dollar, you get: one paper cup, coffee packet, and a can of Sterno!"

AIR TRAFFIC CONTROLLER JOKES

(Although we highly respect these folks, once in awhile, it's nice to poke fun at them).

Air Traffic Controllers use software like SAFE (SPACING AIR-PLANES FOR EXCITEMENT) to help them with landing order and runway assignment. The main glitch in the software is that the capability of the pilot is not factored into the equation so often times passengers taking over for the unconscious pilot are given overly technical directions which are useless to them.

You can tell early on which children would make great air traffic controllers. They're the ones that remember all the ingredients in every cocktail daddy has for breakfast; can't watch Rose Bowl Parade without wincing painfully at dangerously crowded float spacing; and never miss an opportunity to replace a simple 'yes' with 'permission granted'.

ATC folks also make good witnesses to car accidents because of their ability to map from memory the visual layout of a crash scene and recount the details of an auto accident in slow motion, 3D, back-wards or forwards, scene by scene play action then sway the jury by melting into an emotional puddle on the witness stand after painfully reliving every terrifying moment of their near miss incident.

3

ATC person to other ATC person: I can't concentrate. It's too quiet in here! Turn up the static!

ATC SCHOOL:

"OK students, let's go over this again! You want to sound really calm when speaking, but always have your eyes wide open and one hand on your forehead."

ATC SCHOOL'S REGULATIONS:

"It's a federal offense to distract the auditor with an amusing 'three stewardesses and a midget valet' story while a fellow controller deletes potentially embarrassing incident reports from their records or testify a the congressional inquest about ATC sometimes encouraging pilots to attempt the elusive triple spiral to earn bonus points for the landing."

To become an ATC person, schooling is about seven months. After that, you have to take a yearly physical, train at a variety of air-ports, and be tested for drugs every six months to be sure you are using high impact, cutting edge, keep-you-UP amphetamines and not that low end Sanka-like stuff they're peddling on the playgrounds these days.'

ATC are generally folks that like to talk to anyone who'll listen— even those whose faces they can only see in the patterns on their bathroom tile.

Only one out of 50,000 people qualify to be an ATC candidate. And only one out of a million want the job. The problem is that usually only 20,000 apply so the odds are really stacked against them.

The burden of having just one mistake on an ATC person's performance record can end their careers. Pilots realize this and always help ATC out when possible by: putting extra quarters in their 'control terminal' before the screen times out; rolling them onto their side after they pass out; picking up the strippers tab at the "kid's birthday party"; loudly declaring

'This was entirely my doing and should in no way reflect negatively upon the performance record of the controller' into the black box just before impact.

TEN TOP SELLING BOOKS
FOR ATC

ATC Euphemisms for Career Burn Out ("My pilot light went out!").

ATC Pick-Up Lines ("Aircraft, you're cleared for the option. Exit at any taxiway. Need to refuel? Or have lunch tray delivered to your cockpit? You know my frequency. Good Day").

ATC Deathbed Confessions ("Get that tape recorder out of my face!").

Ways to Tell Right From Left ("Mind blowing exercises, industry secrets, and hot tips!").

Responses to Near-Miss Incidents ("Whew! I hope the food cart was secured!").

Clues The Aircraft Is Having A Wild Party On Board (Captain seems preoccupied and discounts the bongo music in the background).

THINGS A DEMENTED PILOT MIGHT SAY ON THE PILOT FREQUENCY OR ANY FREQUENCY FOR THAT MATTER

- Are you a heavy smoker or do you normally sound this way?

- Fellow aviators, our greatest honor as a Kamikaze is to inflict damage on the enemies of the Empire. Muahaha!

- Guess what! My kid is flying me from the ground by remote control.

- Hey, make sure your coffee lid is on good and tight. They sometimes pop open when they're upside down.

- I just decided to quit smoking this morning, so keep a close eye on me now that I have the controls.

- I've had enough of straight and level flight; I think it's time to move on to 'The Mixer'.

- I'll count to 10 and we'll all sing happy birthday.

- Her lawyer says she's gonna get the house, the dog and the kids, there's really nothing for me to look forward to anymore except being up here with you guys.

AIRPLANES: NOW AND IN THE FUTURE

In Japan, Origami Airlines folded after it's first year in operation. It's colorful fleet, lightweight construction, and crease-on-dotted line engineering made passengers uneasy regardless of the low fares and bento box lunches.

Many Japanese citizens come to the US to learn to fly because of cost considerations. In Japan, it must cost about two million yen to learn to fly. In the US, they can learn to fly and have plenty left-over to invest in American real estate.

Airplanes of the future will travel in hyperspace, but if not careful, get stranded in strange dimensions with no way to return unless they leave $100 hamburger crumbs behind.

Most GPS systems don't work as well as hoped! Pilots can program them to find Kansas but not their pens or flashlights!

The earthly sensations of landing are: having to work the yoke a little harder, experiencing pressure in the ears, and feeling the ole butt settle in the seat. The latter is the force that really lands the plane.

Pilots should be well nourished before a flight, but should rule out cannibalism.

Pilots love those new lightweight-folding bikes that weigh only three pounds and can be tossed in their flight bags. The only trouble is finding the bike amongst all that flight gear later.

Every pilot has a fright flight at least once in their flying careers. This is the kind of flight that keeps you grounded for a while until you get your courage back up. Getting back into the cockpit right away is important. Here are seven ways to rebuild confidence:

1. Admit it. They were some flags you ignored. Like the warning of the possibility of "convective activity" along your route.

2. Go over flags with another pilot who won't write about you for an aviation magazine scoop.

3. Let your spouse or significant other know about what happened so they won't think you're moping around the house because of something they did.

4. Review things you could have improved or prevented about the flight from the time you made that idiotic decision to go ahead with it anyway.

5. Find something relaxing to get your mind off those scary after thoughts. Tune into one of those dysfunctional afternoon talk shows where people are flying across the stage after being tossed by bouncers.

6. Pick a challenging day to climb back into the cockpit and don't make the same dumb mistakes twice because now you really know better.

7. Prepare yourself mentally and physically and spiritually. Listen to bedside meditation of seagulls along the seashore.

STEWARDESS FLIGHT LOG

Flight Attendant's Log:

7:00, Entered plane at Co-pilot spent night sleeping in cockpit again. Rousted Co-pilot and his girlfriend from first class

7:03, Brought Co-pilot a Handi-Wipes & coffee then spritzed Co-pilot with Scent Of Leather.

7:15, Food services arrived and tossed 103 teeny-tiny bags of pretzels to me through the emergency exit. I guess I can count that as my aerobic activity for the day.

7:25, Co-pilot's girlfriend upset to find out she hadn't joined the Mile High Club. Asked me to spritz Co-pilot again.

Flight Attendant's Log cont'd:

At 7:30, removed old papers, trash, and stomach linings left by previous passengers.

7:32, Put on a couple pots of coffee. Couldn't remember which one was decaf, but it probably won't really matter.

7:38, Rest of flight crew arrives. Captain still hasn't sprung for lunch even after that last bad landing where we bounced three times, once over another plane, then skidded to a halt.

Flight Attendant's Log cont'd:

7:39, Passengers started boarding. Only a third of them appear to be surly or PMSing. That's much better than the last flight, except for the landing.

7: 46, I spy me a laptop, cell phone, and bagels.

7:52, Check all passengers to make sure seat belts are fastened. Tried to calm nervous passenger with control issues.

Flight Attendant's Log cont'd:

8:45 Stomped on floor several times to let galley know to begin heating up food.

10:30 Told hyper passenger, after drinking too much decaf, to run up and down aisle and quite rearranging luggage in overhead compartment. Guess I know which pot of coffee is the decaf.

11:45 Cleaned up lunches after forgetting to put brake on food cart after severe turbulence. Coffee drinker big help scraping food off cabin's ceiling.

Flight Attendant's Log cont'd:

3:45, Made sure first class passengers had their seat belts fastened for them for landing and gave them each a steamed hand towel, breath mints, and facial spritz.

4:15, Announced to all other passengers to fasten seat belts for landing. Checked to make sure all trays and seat were in upright position. Passed out towelettes and leftover peanut packets.

4:30, Said good-bye to all passengers and thanked coffee drinker for all her help and exchanged emails with her.

THE ALTIMETER

The altimeter is one of the most important instruments on any aircraft. And pilots have a lot in common with them:

- If neglected, altimeters are prone to misbehave.

- Altimeters have a face and hands.

- Altimeters need a point of reference to get on the right track.

- On occasion, altimeters have been known to lie a little depending upon their age or circumstances.

- Altimeters feel less pressure when flying on sunny days because it helps them unwind.

- Altimeters are not influenced by what's printed in the tabloids.

THE PILOT'S WATCH

This would be the kind of watch that would have everything a pilot needs on the ground and in the air.

- A wind sensor that can also pick up Frappucino trails.

- Back up airspeed indicator that works by sticking the watch out the window so that the pinhole port can get a blast of air through it to spin the mini counter wheel.

- Mini nav/com that distorts your voice so badly that ATC grants you immediate permission to land so they won't get a headache listening to you.

- Lots of fancy dials to glance at when the terrain gets boring.

Here is an imaginary dialogue between a cargo aircraft and ATC. The aircraft is bound for Portland International but has just spotted a UFO whilst enroute. The captain is reluctant to report his sighting for fear of getting his license suspended.

5:30:16 W8XXT: (very broken communication; unintelligible) ATC, traff...WOW...bright...aircraft...

5:30:20 ATC: W8XXT, you're coming in broken. Say again.

5:30:23 W8XXT: Request, ah, deviate, ah, ah, from, ah, aircraft with bright lights, ah, request new heading.

5:30:52 ATC: W8XXT, Roger. Fly heading zero zero niner. Deviations approved as necessary to avoid traffic. Traffic not visible on radar.

5:30:49 W8XXT: Roger. Descending to flight level three five zero. Affirmative. Traffic in sight.

5:30:52 ATC: W8XXT, transmission weak.

5:30:56 W8XXT: We see, ah, a very quite big, ah, plane ur um ship at our twelve o'clock. Very bright lights.

5:30:52 ATC: W8XXT, say again. Broken transmission. We received "aircraft at your twelve o'clock"?

5:32:07 W8XXT: (Clearer transmission) Request immediate descent.

5:32:20 ATC: W8XXT approved to flight level three one zero. Descend at pilot's discretion. Maintain flight level three one zero.

5:32:39 W8XXT: Roger. Descend. Maintain flight level three one zero.

5:32:41 ATC: W8XXT, transmission now clearer but we're not picking up your transponder. Please reset.

5:32:45 W8XXT: Affirmative. Transponder reset.

(During the descent, a bump is felt. The pilot and co-pilot are startled.)

5:38:55 ATC: W8XXT, where is your reported traffic now?

5:38:57 W8XXT: Ah, [unintelligible] right below us.

5:39:01 ATC: W8XXT say again? Transmission broken and weak.

5:39:04 W8XXT: Ah, we've made initial physical contact with traffic it appears. **Off Mic:** Unless that was some turbulence we just experienced.

5:39:01 ATC: W893T, what's your position?

5:39:04 W8XXT: WE [emphatically] are right over Salem Airport and inbound for a possible formation landing.

5:39:10 ATC: W8XXT, we received you clearly that time. [Background laughter carries with transmission]. At your discretion proceed to runway 28R through downtown, make right traffic. Keep it tight. Over to 118.9. Good day.

5:39:04 W8XXT: Runway 28R, right traffic. 118.9.

PILOT TO COPILOT: "Next time we won't even try to explain things."

Student pilot challenge
Unusual case scenarios

Challenge 1:

"Hypothetically what would you do if the carb heat knob broke off whilst in flight?" asked the CFI.

"That would depend," answered the Student Pilot cautiously "but I would adjust my RPM to be in the safe zone and land as soon as practicable.

"Very good," remarked the CFI.

Student pilot challenge...
Unusual case scenarios

Challenge 2:

"And what would you do if you saw the amp gauge needle swing wide left whilst enroute?" asked the CFI.

Student pilot said a little more confidently, "I'd turn off the radio and other electrical equipment and inspect; land as soon as practicable."

"Excellent," bellowed the CFI.

Student pilot challenge
Unusual case scenarios

Challenge 3:

"Now, what would you do if the right aileron flew off in flight?" asked the CFI.

The student pilot hesitated for a moment then said, "I'd have you stick your kneeboard out the window and hold it relative to the wind at 20 degrees."

PILOT ERROR

Pilots are human and make mistakes now and then. Here are the more common mistakes.

- Checks comparator to see if turn indicator working properly only after heated debate with co-pilot.

- Reads E6B incorrectly during flight planning and miscalculates aircraft weight as two pounds seven ounces.

- Lands at hangar 51 after reading sectional upside down.

- Believes the glare shield is really a transitional lens. The lower part is great for reading tail numbers, and the upper part for spotting traffic.

- Decides a half-mile separation is enough of a margin between him and his ex-wife.

STEWARDESS: THINGS NOT TO SAY OVER THE INTERCOM

Hmmmmm...I wonder what that noise is.

If you're too stupid to buckle your own seat belt you don't deserve to walk away from the crash.

In case of a water landing, forget the seat cushion, grab someone from the First Class cabin. They tend to float a lot better because they're stuffed with cookies and wine.

THINGS NOT TO SAY OVER THE INTERCOM cont'd:

Please try to be quiet, the pilot can hear you all the way up to the cockpit.

Federal regulation prohibits dismantling of the bathroom smoke detector and running naked through the center aisle screaming, "I need a cigarette and I need one now!"

I think we took off before those folks in the galley could board.

THINGS NOT TO SAY OVER THE INTERCOM cont'd:

In just a few minutes we'll be coming through with the beverage service. If you'd like an alcoholic beverage, please be ready with exact change, a photo I.D., and written permission from your AA sponsor.

I wonder what this red button does?

The oxygen masks have all been filled with nitrous oxide so you'll be laughing hysterically thinking the unscheduled landing is like a Twister party.

We've been cleared for takeoff, so please turn off all cell phones, electronic equipment, and your belief that big metal things can't fly.

GENERAL COMMERCIAL AVIATION JOKES

We're experiencing low visibility this morning. The pilot just came back from the eye doctor and his pupils are still dilated.

The last flight I was on, they had to divert the plane during take-off due to icing conditions. Apparently, one of the baggage handlers tossed out a Big Gulp on the runway.

GENERAL COMMERCIAL
AVIATION JOKES

It's amazing what people will try to put in the overhead compartments. Last week, I caught a woman trying to stuff her husband and three kids in there.

I feel sorry for air traffic controllers because most pilots are men and everyone knows men don't like to ask directions. "Use Runway 17 for landing." "Hey, I'll land where I want to land, I don't need anyone to tell me where to go!"

GENERAL AVIATION JOKES

The only difference flying a stunt plane and flying a passenger plane is that you're the only one who throws up when doing death-defying spirals in a stunt plane.

They used to give passengers metal wings when they flew. Now they give them flak jackets.

GENERAL COMMERCIAL AVIATION JOKES

Flight attendant—the only job where you can go everywhere and nowhere at the same time.

Not everyone has what it takes to become a pilot—a love of adventure, willingness to put in the hours training, and a compulsion to overcome a fear of flying.

TWO PILOTS HAVING A CONVERSATION

===============================

"You can't beat aluminum and rivets," pilot Bill said.

"I like composite aircraft. No rivets or rust," replied pilot Bob.

"Aluminum gives you better crash protection!" pilot Bill countered.

Pilot Bob pondered for a moment, "I still like the part about no rivets or rust."

THE STUDENT PILOT

Beginning student pilots always have questions or remarks when they're starting their flight training. Here are just a few.

Did one person design all of the main gauges in the C-172 or was it like group effort?

You want me to practice what? Sit in a Lazy Boy chair and play with my joystick?

Come on. I beg you. How do you keep the airplane from wiggling on the runway while on the take off roll?

Well, stalls may be the least stressful maneuver on an aircraft, but not on me!

Yeah, sure I know this stuff on the ground, but once I'm up there flying, the only things I can remember are the things I forgot.

(To CFI) Hey, I'm also coping with the fear of flying and claustro-phobia and cramps! So give me a break.

Did you say fright check? You did mean flight check, didn't you?

Can you go over that Density Altitude stuff again.

STUDENT PILOT REBUTTALS

- After a wisecrack from the instructor, the female helicopter student pilot casually replied, "You know, men are just like helicopters, you have to apply constant pressure to keep them going in the right direction."

- (Student pilot to CFI): Okay, that's enough demonstrating. It's my turn to fly the plane.

- (Student pilot to ATC): Hey! That approaching aircraft is daring us to play chicken!

- (Student pilot to CFI): And why can't I land on the roof of that RV? The regs don't say anything about that.

- (Student pilot to CFI): What, specifically, DID you like about my flying today? There must have been something? How 'bout my remembering to keep my eyes open on the landing?

- (Student pilot to CFI): No free soda. Thanks, I'll take my debriefing straight!

- (Student pilot to CFI): I work with computers all day. Looking outside the aircraft is going take some work.

FINDING THE PERFECT
BALANCE...

Flying is a combination of skill, gamble, chance and luck. Everyone who flies knows the risk even though flying is safer than driving.

It stands to reason that if a pilot flew everyday, he/she may be exposed to greater risk of being involved in an incident or accident. So the rule of moderation of don't go pushing your luck, applies to all pilots: Take days off when given, don't volunteer for overtime, and take a train or RV on your vacation as mode of transportation.

FIELD OF DREAMS (SACRED GROUND)

Retired pilots know which runway surface lines not to cross.

REALLY CORNY AVIATION
JOKES

1. What will happen if you let a teething baby fly an airplane?

   You'll get a pilot wail

2. One couple, who met in ground school, decided to get married at their training airport. Friends quipped that the bride should be dubbed "The Runway Bride."

3. How many pilots does it take to change a light bulb?

   It depends on prevailing winds (from wife)...cloud base (how foggy the pilot is) and absolute altitude of light bulb above the ground.

4. Why did the airplane fly inside the concert hall while the symphony orchestra was performing?

   To attempt an instrument landing in a congested area.

5. Why did the pilot leave his checklist at home?

   Because he wanted to wing it.

DIFFERENCES BETWEEN MALE AND FEMALE PILOTS

There's an ongoing debate about women pilots having a higher number of accidents than men even though the ratio of women to men pilots is lower. But if women were really less capable than male pilots, they would be flying only to:

- Tip the joystick only to watch the spinny things move.

- Angle the aircraft to get a reflection off the wing to apply make up.

- Invert the aircraft to tease their hair.

The largest cognitive gender differences are found in visual-spatial abilities. Research shows that males have greater visual-spatial skills than females. But if this were truly a major factor regarding flight...

- Statistically, every third female pilot wouldn't be landing—period.

Males, they say, also tend to be superior in the quantitative area, while females tend to have better verbal skills.

- Maybe that's why women's flight plans look more like an EKG! But at least they are getting to their destinations and landing safely. That's what really counts!

Cognitive performance and spatial abilities are among the most important attributes of flying.

- And young women of today are told they can do anything they want to so many of them are taking more math and science courses and outdoing males on SAT scores, but parallel parking still gives women the most trouble.

Verbal skills are also important to maintain safe air traffic control communication and facilitate crew coordination

- That's why it pays to have a woman in the cockpit with a male pilot. She can tell ATC where to go with their take off and landing instructions.

WHAT WOMEN HAVE SAID ON THEIR SOLO FLIGHT

3x's, orgasmically: "I'm...I'm...flying!"

"It's sure nice and quiet up here without hubbie or the kids."

"I've never thought I'd make it this far. Just goes to show you the power of saying NEVER to a peri-menopausal woman."

"Let's crank it up a notch!"

"OOPS! I think the VOR antenna just snapped off or was that a strap?"

"Let's see...was that one or two landings so far. I'm having so much fun I forgot to count."

"Flying was the best gift to myself after getting that long overdue divorce. Better than getting the house in the divorce settlement."

"They don't call me compass Rosie for nothing!"

AVIATION WISDOM

"Now that you're nearing your check ride," said the instructor to his student, "it's time for the ultimate flying lesson."

The student perked. "What'd you have in mind?"

Five seconds later...

"My plane," barked the instructor when the student froze increasing back pressure on the yoke.

Once back to straight and level flight, the student pilot replied hysterically, "Don't ever try that spin maneuver again!"

Smiling, the instructor said, "You just experienced an important part of your flight training: "Finding the horizon while learning to let go. That's ZEN in a nutshell."

TEN WAYS TO FIGURE OUT WHERE THE WIND IS COMING FROM

Before take off and before landing, a pilot should always check the windsock to see which way the wind is blowing. But if they windsock is not available or clearly visible, here are some tips:

- Fly over an RV park and see which way the underwear or beach towel or catch-of-the-day are flapping on the clothesline.

- Phone a friend and ask: "Hey, which way is the cat fur flying?"

- Ask a passenger to toss a dollar bill out the window.

- Turn on the radio and listen on the pilot frequency for PIREPS like: "I nearly got blown into the next galaxy."

- Fly over Walmart and see which way the helium balloons are headed.

- Phone a golf caddie in a very important golf tournament in your area. They take into consideration every little factor that could affect the path of a golf ball during a crucial putt.

HOW DO YOU KNOW YOUR FLIGHT ISN'T GOING AS PLANNED

1. During preflight, the wind suddenly picks up and takes the plane with it leaving you behind.

2. After take off, the directional gyro keeps pointing back towards the airport.

3. You accidentally squawk 5500 in your transponder on your 55th birthday.

4. A nasty pilot does the "muahaha" evil throaty laugh over the airwaves when you ask for a radio check.

5. One of your legs involves flying over rocky terrain and the airport indicated on your sectional for refueling was just decimated by an avalanche according to a 'just in' PIREP.

6. You get a call on your cell phone and it's your boss telling you to come to work just after you've reached cruising altitude.

7. The person in the co-pilot seat you're taking flying keeps complaining about turbulence when you haven't even taken off.

8. The fuel attendant where you landed asks you to join him for milk and cookies.

9. You forget to close your flight plan on time and the search party decides to take another stab at finding Amelia Earhart.

10. The friend you decided to take flying gets airsick and barfs all over your new polo shirt—causing you to barf all over your new pants.

11. The crop circle you're flying over spells out: IF YOU'RE READING THIS, YOU'RE LOST. TRY A HEADING OF 320 DEGREES. FOOD & FUEL.

12. The last person who rented the aircraft ate fried chicken in the cockpit and greased up all the critical knobs making it extremely difficult to pull the carb heat out during engine roughness.

13. In flight, a plane tailgates you and the pilot tells you all the things you're doing wrong starting with your radio calls, altitude, pattern procedures.

14. Your co-worker has no concept of two-way av talk and doesn't acknowledge receiving your important email to tell the boss, when he gets in, that you're going flying for the rest of the day but will make up the missed time later in the evening to meet the deadline—and so you're constantly wondering, while flying, whether or not your boss thinks he picked the right person for the high profile assignment.

COMMERCIAL AIRLINES

Ever wonder why commercial airlines pack floatation gear for flights over land? You'd think carrying aspirin & ankle wraps would make better usage of space.

And the flight attendant's cheerful voice trailed over the intercom as the passengers evacuated the aircraft: "And don't forget to hold onto your floatation devices while you 'freefall' onto terra firma."

THE OLD DAYS

With all the security around airport these days, it's not like the old days. These days you have to have the right stuff: gobs of ID, lots of patience, and clean socks.

Now the friendly skies has a peeping Tom. A fancy GPS system that tracks all aircraft, even the radio powered ones.

Nowadays, passengers have to be prepared for just about anything on a flight. New airline advertising slogans are saying things like:

- You may get shot down for the sake of national security, so we're going to start serving real food just in case it's you last meal.

- Our flights may have LIVE entertainment on board.

- Martial arts master? Fly first class free!

- Your vacation, in contrast, wouldn't seem like heaven if we didn't mistreat you!

- Fly the airline that offers cockpit celebrities like the 'joined-at-the-hip' twins, mother-daughter duo, and retired actors turned aviators.

FLYING WITH A FRIEND

The next time you take someone flying, I hope they appreciate the gesture, because of all the things you, the PIC, has to do to prepare for flight like check your flight gear and make sure you have what you need and that your references are current, research the weather, review things you might be rusty at, do some flight planning if going on a cross country, drive to the airport, get the plane out of the hangar, preflight the plane, fuel it (and add oil if need be), load your flight gear onto the aircraft, do your run up, take off, make your radio calls, watch for traffic, fly safely and abide by the regulations...

AVIATION FASHION: WOMEN WORKING THE RUNWAY

ENDLESS RUNWAYS

Every pilot has the desire to land at as many runways as possible throughout their flying career. Here are several reasons why:

- Better than mowing the lawn.

- To experience that perfect landing where you don't even feel the touchdown or hear a chirp—just the concussive applause from passengers.

- Because they're hooked—and can't stop without someone's loving support.

- Increased chances of bumping into Goldie Hawn and Kurt Russell.

- Because finding airports in the midst of concrete jungles are half the fun. "There, two o'clock position, one mile, that's two points for me and none for thee!"

"HOW LOST IS LOST?"

The pilot did a double take on his gauges and realized he was getting low on fuel so he climbed to a higher altitude and got on the radio:

PILOT

"ATC...I'm unsure of my position. 64XX"

ATC

"64XX, Squawk 5X2X"

PILOT

(Beat)
"Squawk 5X2X . Roger 64XX"

ATC

(Responds in a few seconds)
64XX, you're two miles Southwest of Cheez and about 10 miles West of Cottage City.

PILOT

(Relieved)
Roger. Thanks. 64XX

ATC

64XX fuel at Cheez or Cottage if needed.

PILOT

Roger. Think I'll pass on Cheez and head for Cottage. 64XX.

ATC

64XX, would you like a side of fruit with that request?

AVIATION TERMS

FORMATION FLYING: Synchronized aeronautical activity that requires precision flying skills and lots of women's intuition.

DROGUE CHUTE: A snagged clothesline or textile canopy that slows an airplane down by providing drag.

TRUE FLYING: Smooth, unhurried flight where your bladder isn't complaining.

YANK, BANK, CHECK MY TANKS: Aerobatic pilot's in-flight check-list while performing blood-curdling maneuvers.

SPAR DING: Dent caused by frustrated student pilot kicking wheel spar after landing so hard CFI chipped tooth.

DUCK SENSE: Realization that you've wondered too far from the goodies.

E5B: Earlier prototype of the E6B that didn't quite make the production line because it kept coming up with answers like 'try again!'

PILOT THINK

When a pilot starts thinking about buying a boat or RV or motorcycle and giving up their aircraft, it's time for group intervention!

One reason pilots like to fly is because of curiosity about clouds and they love darting through them because it's more fun than poking a wooden stake through artificial fog from one of those Halloween contraptions.

Grass Airports! They can be a bear to mow, which is why pilots invented the sport of lawn mower drag racing with pit crews to empty collecting bags and refuel the mowers.

The pure joy of open cockpit flying executing 80 degree turns, death spirals, and pitchovers was reworded to: "Feel the wind through your hair, get a bird's eye view, and soar through the clouds"—to increase business.

ABOUT AIRPORTS

SKULL ROCK RUNWAY:

Runway: part gravel, part quick sand, part dirt. Edges marked with spray painted pinecones. Sexually active livestock present on heavily pitted runway. Caution: railroad cars make the centerline. No 'go arounds' due to steep terrain. Stop and go not worth damage to aircraft. Buzzards at the end of the runway just waiting for a mishap.

LONER'S LANDING:

Runway 17 extremely cracked and distressed. Inexperienced pilots should not land here, period. Helicopters welcome at all times. Caution: feral cats darting across runway chase by retired vet with large syringe. Cattle feeding in grassy areas around displacement and runway center. Windsock midfield behind rickety shack. Gopher holes throughout primary surface. They don't call this runway Loner's Landing for nothing.

PEACE STRIP:

Active protestors in lotus position marking runway edges. A giant peace sign signifies runway threshold. Right traffic. VASI (people holding political signs). Windsock made from hemp. Distances marked with tie dye shirts.

YOUNG GIRLS WHO BECAME PILOTS

Encouraged everyone, including dad, to wear blue eye shadow.

Wanted airplane rides—not pony rides—for their birthdays.

Dreamed of one day owning an Amanda Airport doll (but no toy company ever invented one).

Have a desire to defy those that tell them 'they can't.'

Wanted to be a pilot—not a stewardess—from the get go.

Found playing with dolls OK but had more fun playing airplane pilot in a cardboard box with brother and his friends.

RULES OF THE AIR

Never skip an item on your checklist unless you're chased by a hostile tribe or a stampede of wild cattle.

When in doubt, do a 360.

The propeller works better when it's spinning really really fast.

They say the trim tab is for relieving pressure off the yoke. And for helping the aircraft maintain airspeed. But we all know the TRIM tab is to keep the nose of the plane pointed upwards especially after the PIC ate too big of a meal before flight.

Always land into the wind unless it's a hurricane.

Pack a flight bag full of gear for ballast.

Keep a sterile cockpit. Focus on flying and maneuvering the aircraft at all times. Refrain from discussing what toppings you ordered on the pizza you had for lunch.

THINGS MALE & FEMALE PILOTS THOUGHT OR SAID WHEN THEY WERE KIDS

When I was a little kid, I used to think that if I ate enough cereal, I'd have enough cereal boxes to build a hangar!

You mean the decals for model planes aren't tattoos?

Why can't Barbie marry G.I. Joe and fly off into the wild blue yonder?

And what do airplane wheels do once they're in the wheel well? Do they keep spinning to make the plane go faster?

My glider got caught in the tree again!

The best thing about going to summer camp are ghost stories, marshmellow roasts, and the airplane ride getting there!

Let's eat French fries at the airport and watch the airplanes! Please! I'll be good.

NO! I don't want to go to Disneyland, I want to go to the airport!!!

I can sound like a gas powered hobby plane when I pinch my nose and go "Eeeeee-vrrooom". Wanna see?

AIRPORTS OF THE FUTURE

What will airports of the future be like?

Airports of the future won't take up gobs of runway like they do now. In the future, planes taking off will do so into large air generating fans that look like giant blow dryers. During the landing phase, planes will glide into mechanically generated headwinds whereby then can set various wind velocities by clicking their PTT buttons.

For maximum climb and landing performance, artificial cooling ducts will make air denser so airplanes taking off or landing will have better and predictable performance.

Airports will be called hairports instead. Taxiways will be turned into lodging and recreation for pilots and passengers where they can dine, get Rex Morgan buzz cuts, and visit aeronautical museums.

INSIGHT FOR STUDENT PILOTS TO REDUCE TRAINING ANGST

Realize that instructors make a lot of mistakes that you are too dumb to pick up on at the moment.

Precision takes practice and doesn't come overnight unless you pay extra.

Relax. Everyone squints to read the dials and gauges.

It takes at least 59 bad landings before instructors tell you about the one little thing you left out to make all the difference.

Your instructor has mastered self-control and won't laugh at your mistakes (promise)—except with other instructors.

So you experienced your first ground loop. Welcome to the club!

Every pilot experiences minor incidents at some time or another in their flying career. Finding a pilot to talk about these incidents is another story.

Instructors will rattle things off sometimes mostly because they know the material so well that it comes natural to them. Don't entertain the thought for a second that it's because they think you've got a photographic memory.

You won't find manuals or instruction booklets for any of the instruments inside your training aircraft because they're carefully stashed away in some grain silo in Nebraska.

Remember, flight instructors have made the same mistakes you have once upon a time and it's a good idea to ask them to share their most memorable moments with you so you won't feel like such a dork for stepping on only one toe brake causing the aircraft to loop around a flag pole fifty times.

CORPORATE PILOTS

Co-pilot: Sir! Can I interrupt...

Captain: Sure. I was just in the middle of a conversation with ATC (unkeys mic).

Co-pilot: Engine number two on our starbird side just lost compression.

Captain: It's a good thing we have one engine left.

Co-pilot: Engine number one fell off on take off.

Captain: (Yawns) I'll inform the tower of our situation.

Co-pilot: What about the passengers?

Captain: Being that we're in a simulator we can walk away from these Stephen King-like scenarios unscathed.

Co-pilot: But what about when we're flying for real?

Captain: The odds are a million to one we'd face a scenario like this one where an evil clown is tampering with our aircraft.

SACRIFICES PEOPLE MAKE TO BECOME...PILOTS

- Student pilot in Montana, in an effort to save on the hourly rental rates of the C-172 trainer, took a ballet class at the nearby college "to get 25% off" the hourly plane rental.

- Student pilot in New Hampshire was gladly accepting "voluntary donations" from family members ``who really believed he was cutting engine power right after take off" to save on gas even though he tried to convince them otherwise.

- Private pilot in Phoenix, seeking her instrument ticket, gave up mocha frappacinos and was surprised to see how much she was saving that she ended up buying her own plane."

- Student pilot in Nevada, an RN getting her private pilot rating, gave up desserts, magazines, and shopping carts.

- Another Private Pilot in Ohio, bid on aviation items on ebay at 3AM in the morning to get the best deals on closing auctions.

- A Private Pilot from Wisconsin, tried to turn sevens into ones on the HOBBS meter claiming paralax error when he eventually got called on it by the FBO's office manager.

- A clever student pilot stood at an intersection with a cardboard sign that read: "Planeless. Will work for fuel. I'll plan your cross-country vacation."

PILOT TO PILOT TALK IN THE COCKPIT

- Do you think we can break the sound barrier with all this luggage?

- We can fly better than birds can. But birds are smarter because they don't push flying in bad weather.

- I don't think cussing at an instrument qualifies it as being a two-way communication device. So, no, we're not legal.

- We're going to be swooping down low on the runway and picking up a few passengers. By the way, how's your Spanish?

- There ought to be a restaurant called Tomato Flames just for pilots.

- Yep, they were the good ole days. We used to do the shake-n-bake. We'd fill Ziploc bags with flour and target ranging chickens from five hundred feet AGL.

- Flying into that electrical storm last May really changed me. Not only am I psychic, but when I go the the grocery store, I generate so much static electricity I can actually warm up a can of spaghetti.

- My worst experience? I spent three days in the desert before help arrived. I munched on sand and licked condensation off a cactus. It was a humbling experience and it's made me a better pilot. Next time, I'll remember to take extra gas along for the car.

- Here, wear this concrete thing around your neck. It's the only fireproof thing on the aircraft in case we don't make it.

- Captain to Co-pilot: "During the in-flight movie, let's attempt a full roll. The passengers will just think they saw the stewardess upside down."

- Just imagine how many round trip cross countries a bee makes without weather briefings, charts, and frappacino. We're spoiled!

- Pretty soon the windows in this cockpit will just be tiny little slits. The airlines want us to focus on the horizon—not the view—to improve flight safety.

NINTENDO GENERATION

Will fly airplanes with their thumbs!

THINGS THAT ONLY OCCUR AT AIRPORTS

The only friendly people are the ones with the shaved heads playing the harpsichord really badly.

Your old high school teacher gives you an A for making the gate on time.

Airport Security asks you about the hickie.

You get a white courtesy telephone call from a telemarketer asking if you'd like to buy traveling insurance.

The baggage porter gives you a ride on his cart when he sees the bags under your eyes.

The car rental clerk offers you the only car available, hers, at double the rate.

The ticket agent, when asking you if you packed your own bags, looks at you strangely when you tell her your cat helped.

THINGS KIDS SAY ABOUT AIRPLANES

Do planes cartwheel like a dirt bikes when they hit a speed bump going too fast on the tarmac?

Mine is going to have swimming pool in it so it can make a splash landing

Why don't logbooks come in the same colors as crayons?

And why are logbooks called logbooks? They're not made out of logs.

PONDERABLE

Flight crew should be called posse. It's not like they walk down the loading ramp wearing space suits and helmets with "The Right Stuff" embroidered on their uniforms.

THE DARNDEST THINGS PILOTS SAY ON THEIR CELL PHONES WHILE FLYING

"I'm must be flying over a yuppie neighborhood because I see a lot of swimming pools."

"Hi—I'm phoning from 10,000 feet and I'd like to order a pizza delivered to Roseburg Airport. My ETA is 2200 Zulu. No, this isn't a crank call."

"What? Say again. I can't hear you over the hum of the engine!"

"Dave, did you know your phone number spells 'Tomato flaps'?"

"ATC, my radio is out and I'm requesting a light show."

"Guess where I'm calling from! No, not the space shuttle, an airplane!"

"Got to go! I've got hail pouring into the cockpit through the air vents."

"Honey, there's still time to look up the number while I do my run up. Hurry."

PILOTS INTRODUCING THEMSELVES TO THE PASSENGERS BEFORE TAKE OFF

"Good afternoon passengers, my name is Captain Douglas Boomer of Cincinnati and I'll be your flight jockey for today. We'll be making a touch down in about six hours. In the mean time, let's gain some yardage by taxiing to the runway."

"Greetings Ladies and Gentlemen, I'm Captain Elijah and we should have a very pleasant flight. Think of the aircraft as a chariot with wings guided by angels."

"Hello and welcome aboard. My name is Captain Burt Dinklemeyerson. Our flight to Boston should take roughly seven hours, and once we reach cruising altitude—let Karaoke hour begin."

"Welcome aboard flight 372. I'm Captain Bob Cloud. We're going to be cruising at an altitude of 100,000 feet where you'll get a good view of the planet. To compensate for landing in Cleveland, our descent rate will be 5,000 fpm after reaching very thin air."

EXPERIMENTAL AIRCRAFT

Manufacturer's suggestion:

To add crash protection to your aircraft, use a high-grade shellac.

Kit ad:

The model X-17-ultra comes with two sets of awnings that attach to the wire frame fuselage. Lawn chairs are extra.

Aircraft manufacturer's warning:

We don't recommend that you test your newly built aircraft right after you've secured the last nut and bolt. Have someone else do it.

We're proud to be a different breed:

We're not afraid to build our dreams and crash into barns testing our designs. Our goal is to build the first balsa wood aircraft to circle the globe.

PILOT SURVIVAL

International flights:

So many pilots get drowsy on international flights that the galley puts pieces of tin foil in the flight crew's food and beverages.

CFI TO STUDENT PILOT

No time to study your FAR/AIM? Well then you're a horrible, horrible student pilot!

Decorating your airplane with pinecones is a sure means of getting your student pilot's license revoked!

Getting your pilot's license will be the proudest day of your life. You'll look back at all your training and realize why I got on your case about little things like putting Velcro strips on your pens, laminating your checklist, and tying your shoelaces.

CAPTAIN TO STEWARDESS

"We've got engine problems and we're low on fuel. Get the passengers as drunk as possible, as early as possible."

SPICING THINGS UP IN THE COCKPIT

- For helicopter pilots, fly an airplane!

- Bring along a pair of high-powered binoculars and fly over a nudist camp.

- Take turns blindfolding one another in the cockpit and pinning post it notes on different instruments.

- Get a bunch of C-172 pilots together and fly in formation over a small town, each plane unrolling a roll of toilet paper to make it look like contrails.

MEMO

TO: TEST PILOT
FROM: ENGINEERING TEAM

With a high aspect ratio, the aircraft has limited maneuverability at slow speeds, due in part, to the heavier-than-air construction. You see, we run out of aluminum and had to use lead.

Best to keep the aircraft at 50 feet AGL until we correct any instability you may encounter. There's a high probability that our calculations are correct except for those by the new recruits from the shipping department.

Enjoy your test flight! Hope to see you at the company picnic next week.

ON THE OTHER SIDE OF THINGS

- **Aviation astrologer (to pilot):** "You've got three things challenging your around the world flight: weather, mechanical problems, and moon wobble. Take you pick."

- **Psychic who reads inside of flight bags—like tea leaves in a cup—telling pilots their future!** "I see a definite pattern! See the way the logbook juxtaposes against the kneeboard. There's a connection there that will reveal itself in due time."

- **Aviation astrologer:** "I recommend all pilots not fly during Mercury retrograde. Planetary shifting does affect mechanical bodies which include aircraft engines and mechanics."

- Favorite discount catalog for pilots: **"Wing Nut."**

- The dog, who accidentally tore up the pilot's logbook, is in the witness protection program.

SURVIVOR PILOT

The new game show where 100 pilots battle it out on an unspoiled island. The winner gets a refurbished vintage aircraft and a year's supply of Calamine lotion.

The Game:

Each pilot tries to land on a short-n-narrow runway, with shark infested waters at both ends, wearing a skin-tight rubber suit with arm wings after getting tossed out of an aircraft from 30,000 feet.

After landing, if intact, pilots search for a chest filled with hamburgers buried under a pile of musty logbooks using vectors tattooed to their wrists

When night falls, the surviving pilots sit around a bonfire and share daring stories of flying adventures. Those with the most logged time form a clique and vote other pilots off the island, by sheer intimidation, at sunrise. Remaining pilots battle it out by engaging in E6B competitions.

PEOPLE SELLING AIRPLANES

Art dealer:

The citation catches your eyes with perfection of its fuselage and wings. With the sensation of flying at 550 KTS at cruising speed, the aircraft holds us with its swept back wings and sleek overall design. Models come in elegant egg-shell with stainless steel chrome trim.

A grocery clerk selling an airplane:

"Did you find everything in the plane today? Should you purchase this model with a coupon, your total comes to $1,000,450.00. Would you like paper or plastic for a barf bag?

A musician selling an airplane:

"This craft comes with a Dolby sound system enclosed in a sound proof cabin! The control system is right under the bar. Have a listen (cranks up the volume and starts foot tapping). (Shouting) This is for entertaining your rich friends at 50,000 feet. Love that syncopation. Hard to find a better aircraft with this kind of sound."

Paula Poundstone selling an airplane:

Let me call an airplane expert on my cell phone and then I'll improvise from there.

THE LATEST STATS ON EJECTION SEATS!

Some ejection seats have over 1300 parts that better doggone work.

Airlines are considering bringing back ejection seats to use on passengers who complain about the food, stale cabin air, and the lousy in-flight movie. Instead of calling them ejection seats, they're calling them "in flight entertainment stations."

Ejections seats were in use a lot during World War II mainly because they didn't have the kinks worked out of the timing mechanism.

Ejection Seats have been used over 12000 times to date but the numbers are decreasing due to having the kinds worked out of them.

When inspected, all functions of an Ejection Seat must work within 1/10 of a second because that's how long it takes a pilot to back out.

Astronauts sat on ejection seats where the handles were stowed in a covered compartment at the base of the seat and voice activated by the words "Oh $@&!"

Early Russian Cosmonauts were required to use ejection seats on their return from space which didn't make them very happy campers considering it was one more terrifying task to do before getting reaching earth.

Some ejection seats are controlled by microprocessors. Some are controlled by remote control on the ground to keep pilots in line.

Some Ejection Seats weigh over 200 lbs. But most of the weight comes from explosives.

Some jets use an explosive to shatter the canopy inches above the pilot's helmet. The canopy cannot be jettisoned, so if the explosive don't work, the ejection seat will punch through it anyway. This design didn't sell too well even though it showed a surviving pilot having beers with his/her buddies on the packaging.

The exact number of female ejectees is increasing as more women are becoming involved in military aviation thanks to clever wording in the recruiting brochures.

Helicopters are also equipped with an egress system that jettison the rotors with an explosion leaving the crew to attach themselves to passing aircraft with suction cups.

Early production aircraft utilized a crew module that ejected the entire cockpit and occupants to descend intact but found that severe turbulence could sometimes activate this option leaving passengers to fend for themselves.

Most egress systems are designed to separate from the crew and allow them to descend under a normal parachute. Crews can select from different types of parachutes depending upon their sense of adventure.

Nose capsules (jettisoning the entire front of the airplane just aft of the cockpit) were explored and used Cabbage Patch dolls as test agents.

THINGS ALL PILOTS HAVE IN COMMON...

A secret wish for the control lock to be made of edible candy.

Dropping things under the seat and not being able to reach it unless they bank 80 degrees or more.

Losing their favorite six-dollar pen in the cockpit.

Wishing someone out there would make the perfect kneeboard and flight bag.

A weakness or two in their flying repertoire for which charm and great aviation talk compensate for.

Forgetting items on the checklist only to remember them after the flight

Wishing ATC didn't have to correct in front of others on read back.

Bad hair days in the cockpit from inverted flight and turbulence.

Being on the wrong frequency and feeling like a dufuss.

PILOT HEAVEN

Where does a pilot do his/her best thinking? If you ask me, it's the best-kept secret on the planet.

Pilots refer to it as reaching 'cut off.' That special altitude that makes a pilot feel like a ghost, detached yet cognizant, relaxed and clear headed. Some of the best ideas and thoughts came to fruition as a result of 'cut off.'

- The cockpit roach. Never lose anything in the cockpit ever again. Accurately emulates real household roaches.

- The twin engine ceiling fan for really hot summer days!

- The inflatable co-pilot that never-slouches or talks back or misreads comparators.

- Headphones that have the ability to instantly replay transmissions so pilots don't have to ask ATC to repeat themselves and look foolish.

- Aircraft that lets you deploy a basement if you land in quicksand. Great for adventure flyers, scientists, and people with money to squander.

ARMCHAIR PILOT'S CHECKLIST

Fixed Wing
Student pilot

- Place a comfortable chair in front of your living room window.

- Use a real or pretend instrument panel depending upon your budget

- Strap kneeboard with checklist to knee

- Go through checklist out loud

- Feel yourself slip into trance while staring into nothingness

- Make radio call to ground for permission to taxi

- Do your run up and take off

- Maintain pattern altitude

- Practice landings and go arounds

When you hear clapping, turn around to see room full of people attending your surprise birthday party and video taping you.

PILOTS AND AGING...

Every pilot wants to fly forever and never grow old. To maintain that youthful look, this is what pilots are doing to stay young both mentally and physically:

- Flying steeper descents to smooth out wrinkles.

- Using middle age spread instead of air bags for crash protection that does wonder for flattening those abs.

- Throwing Hobbs meter milestone parties with flying buddies right on tarmac.

- Spritzing collected cloud vapor on crow's feet.

- Flying higher altitudes to lessen the effects of gravity.

- Attempting daring maneuvers in their dreams.

- Switching to low calorie cockpit snacks such as snowcones made from hail coming through air vents with Sweet-n-Low sprinkled on top.

- Planning on being pilots in the next go around.

PILOTS & CAMPING

COMMERCIAL PILOTS:

When a commercial pilot goes camping, it's usually because of an unscheduled landing in the woods.

BUT WHEN PRIVATE PILOT'S GO CAMPING...

(They are eager to share their stories with you. Here's one!).

The bumpiest ride of my life wasn't flying in rough turbulence but landing in a cow pasture.

In my nifty aircraft, you only need 15 yards to land her as long as you have the skill to make numerous quick u-turns for the roll out.

I bought a loaf of bread at the campground store but could not find my all-in-one knife in flight bag to spread the peanut butter and jelly—so I toughed it out and went hungry.

Set up sleeping bag under the wing of plane. Good thing. Rained throughout the night. Temperature dropped from 80 degrees Fahrenheit to 30 degrees Fahrenheit.

Home looked real good at this point.

I put myself in a hypnotic trance by staring at the encroaching fog to forget about my stabbing hunger pangs and the cold. I thought about the rules of flying near mountains: engage in slow flight for recon of terrain, approach ridges at 45 degree angle, and think ahead of the aircraft by remembering to pack spare utensils.

FYI, do not take off with open door and window unless everything is secured. Lost peanut and jelly and loaf of bread on rotation but found all-in-one knife hiding beside base of seat.

Fortunately, I had heard about a breakfast at a nearby reservation from other hungry campers . Headed there and ate for a whole hour to make up for no dinner. Washed dishes later because credit cards and check flew out the door during last take off.

BUT WHEN PRIVATE PILOT'S GO CAMPING cont'd:

Very glad to return home.

Logbook entry: Total time 5.23 hours, average ground speed 101 knots, distance covered 75 nautical miles, fuel burn about 7.50 gals per hour and oil used was 9.5 liters.

DISCOVERY FLIGHT

There's a good reason why flight instructors take folks on Discovery Flights. Read the dialog below:

Student: "I think you'd be a great instructor for me, but I've got reservations about continuing..."

Instructor: "Oh?"

Student: "Tell me, what is emotionally appealing to you about flying?"

Instructor: (Pauses) "Learning to do things properly, learning all this is necessary for safe flight, seeing the world from another perspective, and engaging in aviation talk. Of course, learning to fly also means having an additional mode of transportation."

Student: "Yeah, aviation talk is cool. But when you did that steep turn, my body didn't know what to do with the G forces. I was ready to give up my lunch. So I thought, I gotta rethink this. Doesn't make sense to eat a lunch then lose it, if you know what I mean?"

Instructor: (Peeks at watch. Thinks about what's for lunch). Yes, I know what you mean. Lunch is an important thing.

Student: "Flying to me feels like surfing on air while paddling a canoe. That's my subjective feedback about the Discovery Flight."

Instructor: (Calmly) "That's an interesting analogy. A first for me."

Student: "I guess what I'm looking for is an adrenaline rush, like motorcycling over a cliff, RV drag racing, pole vaulting over a canyon. I spend all day behind a boring computer, programming. I'm ready for an extreme adventure when I get off work."

Instructor: (Smiles) "Well, thanks for your honesty. I'm glad the Discovery Flight helped you identify what you're really after. A death wish."

A LOT OF OLDER PEOPLE QUIT FLYING AFTER THEY SOLO. HERE ARE SIX REASONS WHY

• Like having someone to chitchat with on solo cross-countries other than hurried and stressed out folk on the radio.

• Lost of dentures while cussing when bending over in cockpit to retrieve heart medication.

• Gravity and having to step up to check the fuel tanks in high wing aircraft.

• Forgetfulness getting in the way of remembering who you are, where you are, and what you want to do.

• Totally spaced out setting goal of getting private pilot license because worried about not seeing enough of the grandchildren.

• Want only a sport license where you race your friends in the pattern.

PILOTS ON AN INTERNATIONAL FLIGHT

Ever wonder what happens on commercial airline flights between the captain and his crew? Read on!

Captain: (To Co-pilot) "I'm ready for a nap. You have the controls."

Co-pilot: "I have the controls." (Pauses) Think I'll watch the meteor shower. I'll have the stewardess make me some popcorn on her next round."

Captain: "I'll make my nap brief. About 20-minutes. Then it's your turn. Afterwards, we can discuss the aircraft over pie and coffee."

Stewardess: (Peeks into cockpit) "How we doing? Are you all awake and functioning? Ready for another dose of caffeine?"

Co-pilot: "I'll take another round of tea. The Captain went down to the starboard wheel well to hibernate."

Flight Engineer: "I'll have a Shirley Temple with a couple of cherries."

Co-pilot: (To stewardess) "The meteor shower is starting!"

Stewardess: "Hey! That one came pretty close."

Flight Engineer: (Perks) "You're right. A couple of hundred feet and it would have dinged us!"

Co-pilot: (Excited) "I'm going to turn off the auto pilot and take her up a new notches."

PERFECT LANDINGS

Seven ways to improve your landings in no time!

1. Try steadying a hot cup of coffee on your dash from final to touchdown.

2. Video tape ducks landing in a pond and replay video footage when no one's home. You'll be amazed at all the things you'll learn from nature's feathery friends, who, by the way, love to ski on the water when they're in the flair.

3. Don't fret about the cost of practicing...you can always get a third job.

4. Keep your eyes focused further down the runway to spot dancing bears.

5. Remind yourself that nobody is watching you screw up.

6. Do what comes natural to avoid smacking the ground: like paying attention.

7. Look for subtle clues to gauge your height above the ground like folks spread-eagle on the ground.

WHAT PILOTS SAY TO OTHER PILOTS

Let me know when we clear 10,000 and are over uncongested terrain. I'd like to toss my sack lunch out the window.

We'll try descending at 3,000 fpm to meet the arrival schedule but there might be a lot of cleaning up in the cabin once we've landed. I'd hate to tarnish our perfect record of delivering passengers to the gate on time. If there's a will, there's a way.

Nope, I've never seen a UFO on any flight, honest.

I brought my checklist this time. See! (uncrumples a sheet of paper)

I can't see a dang thing out of these itty-bitty windows as it is without your starchy big hairdo getting in the way.

I think one of the scaly monsters got out of the cargo crates.

Whatever we're hauling back there, I don't wanna know.

I once saw a cloud that looked like George Washington's hair.

No, we're not landing there. That airport doesn't have frappucino.

I gave the cargo a good shove towards the aft. That should angle us perfectly.

I'd opt for leaving that loud sales person behind rather than dump 20 gallons of fuel.

DIVERSIONS TACTICS TO SLOW TRAFFIC ENTERING THE PATTERN

"BravoXXWhiskey...here's yet another hand off."

"Traffic entering the 45, you might want to hold off entering the pattern until you've flown over the magnificent terrain just two miles west of a 305 degree heading."

"Make a 360 then a 1-minute vertical into a spiral descent prior to entering the pattern."

"First aircraft to answer how many fingers I'm holding up can enter the pattern."

"Caution, ricocheting wake turbulence"

"Check your belongings and make sure you've got everything. It's not too late to turn back."

"We're breaking to do a shift change. Be back shortly."

RICHARD SIMMONS EXERCISE VIDEO FOR PILOTS

The new exercise video called TAKE OFF. Slim away extra baggage that's between you and that that yoke!

Work out at your nearest airport already designed like a workout gym replete with other out-of-shape people, snack bars, and sweaty clothes (packed in suitcases) to give you that authentic gym aroma.

• Exercise those flabby thighs and buns on the luggage conveyor belt.

• Run up the down the escalator using passengers as resistance to tone leg and shoulder muscles.

• Carry your own baggage for a cardiovascular workout.

• Sprint to different gates to work those inner thigh muscles.

• Stand on the runway centerline and dodge planes while moving in beat with flashing runway lights while listening to your favorite tunes.

• Help airport security catch running suspects.

This exercise video workout is guaranteed to help you lose those extra pounds while working out in your favorite pilot environment without the restriction of the cockpit where you might injure a fellow pilot and get sued. Hit tunes include: UP UP AND AWAY, LEAVING ON A JET PLANE, JET AIRLINER, FLY ME TO THE MOON, SATISFACTION, GO CHICKEN FAT GO, AND MORE!

PILOT PET PEEVES

- Yappy passengers

- Yappy co-pilot

- Yappy spouses

- Yappy dogs

- Yappy air traffic controllers

SIMPLE COMFORTS PILOTS FIND INDISPENSABLE TO THEIR WELL BEING

- A weather briefing with a positive outlook.

- A happy memory of their mothers.

- Their soon-to-be ex-spouse removed from the passenger list.

- A five minute cuddle with their favorite fuzzy cockpit pal.

- An inspirational reading from the Koran.

- A sensible pump with a modest heel.

ABOUT SOME ADVENTUROUS PILOTS

Like to work for Fed-Ex parcel service because they prefer the conversation with the passengers remain on that level.

Frequently tempt co-pilot to push red 'CARGO EJECT' button on long mail runs.

Instruct fuel attendants to subtract 25 gallons from whatever the minimum fuel range listed by the POH.

Refer to their therapists as 'baggage handlers.'

Have new carpet the floor under their pedals every 100 hours.

Have posters of well-known aviators gracing the cabin of his plane!

Makes his/her passengers feed him/her an in-flight snack!

Flies as a refreshing break from job as an NYC cabbie.

Insists on making a good first impression and orders co-pilot to clean bugs from windshield with squeegee before every landing.

Informs passengers that lost luggage is one of the unfortunate risks of air travel, but fails to mention that sometimes only certain items in your bags may turn up missing like a pink angora sweater.

Likes to pin the aviator wings on his younger passengers with a powerful arcing down stroke and a chilling, resonant laugh

Tells passengers that seatbelts are listed as an upgrade option in their 'happy flier' flight package.

Believes that without god there would be no pilots, but believes that without pilots, there would be no god so therefore pilots are really important.

Prefers the flight simulator program to his job because the computer doesn't recoil in horror and swear in retaliation when he banks 90 degrees.

Enjoy playing the in-flight movie that features a loop of NTSB crash site footage with 'YOU ARE HERE' arrow cleverly edited into the frames.

Doesn't flinch with several near miss incidents attributed to his lack of attention while mentally calculating crosswind component.

Take up the challenge when ATC lights two strands of swim buoys on a nearby lake and defers him to 'Auxiliary Runway 7' during a recent attempted night landing.

Knows that women ATC often breathe 'I should be so lucky' (as their hearts race with hopeful anticipation) when he announces he's on 'final approach.'

EPILOGUE

Thanks for purchasing this book. This was a fun project!

I've added a couple of things to the very end as optional reading for those of you who like to read.

If you're a student pilot, don't give up on your training when the training gets tough. Find things to laugh about and get through the difficult challenges. You'll be glad you did. Because that's what builds character.

Best,
Core F. Keller

THE TAXI WAY

Short Story

By Core F. Keller

One morning, as I was taxiing to runway 35, about a hundred yards ahead of my C-172, was a dog-like figure crossing the taxiway making its way into the dry brush. At first, I thought it was some-one's lost dog. As I got closer, I realized it was a coyote, probably looking for a morning meal before the scorching sun reared its blazing head.

I spotted the animal sitting in the grass and eyeing the aircraft as it rolled by. It's pelt showed a great variety of color. Light brown-ish grays to buff colors with soft under fur in contrast to the coarse texture of its fur. It's broad pointed ears perked at the sound of the aircraft's revving powerplant while its yellow eyes paid me careful vigilance.

As I did my run up just a few feet away, the coyote kept its posi-tion. I could sense the animal was watching the aircraft taxi onto to the runway.

That was the last I saw of the coyote until a few days later, when I was headed out to take some aerial photographs of Clear Lake.

This time, however, I saw the coyote just a few feet from the run up area. I nearly missed him if it weren't for catching sight of his pinkish brown tongue hanging out of its mouth. More than likely, his prey was in the nearby vicinity. But for some reason, I was hoping the animal had recognized my aircraft and was making an attempt to connect with me.

I could feel the animal's gaze as I methodically went through my checklist. When I was done and was headed for the runway, my wingtip was now only twenty feet abreast of the animal. And we made eye contact. I stared into the yellows eyes for what seemed like an interminable minute. Then I made my radio call and took off.

I did not see the coyote the next time I went flying since I had taken to flying in the afternoons because of my work schedule. It wasn't until two weeks later that the opportunity to return to morning flying materialized, and I was eager to see if the coyote would be around.

There was no sign of the animal along the taxiway or run up area. As I began my take off roll, giving the aircraft full throttle, I felt a slight disappointment. When I had reached the proper altitude to turn left crosswind and began banking to the west, I saw a pack of coyotes in a nearby watermelon field where they appeared to be feeding on the farmer's crop for lack of something better to eat.

Mark Twain had once said, "The coyote "is a living, breathing allegory of Want. He is always hungry. He is always poor, out of luck and friendless. The meanest creatures despise him and even the fleas would desert him."

But for those brief moments, it seemed comforting to have the coyote's companionship on the lonely taxiway.

THE JET SETTERS

The soap opera that never made the airways...

Karen: Flight attendant, 29
Travis: Steward, 31
Captain: Bill, 32
First Officer: Mike, 32
Galley manager: cameo appearances by aging actors
Pilot's Wife: Shirley, 32

SCENE 1:

(Stewardess and Steward are preparing the plane prior to the passengers boarding)

Karen: I spritzed aisle 23, seat 23B. One of the passengers must have puked the pasta meal we served yesterday.

Travis: (Sighs) That's because the Captain hasn't been maintaining altitude. On yesterday's flight, we went from 30,000 to 50,000 back to 30,000.

Karen: The Captain has a lot on his mind. His flight physical is coming up and I think there's trouble in the bedroom.

Travis: I forgot to tell you about one of the passengers forgetting to put his tray in the upright position so I deducted brownie points from his overall score. I tampered with latch to the bathroom door so while the passenger was in it and the plane lurched, well, guess who tumbled out.

Karen: Is that the same passenger sitting by the emergency exit door? Do you think he's capable, you know, if we need him during a real emergency?

Travis: (Laughs) The woman that passed out in row 36, seat B. Three valiums and Saint Bernard drool. She was low turbulence all the way to Chicago. That's my kind of passenger. Total zombie.

(Cabin fills with robust laugher).

Karen (looks at watch): Well the rest of the crew should be arriving any minute now. I can hear the luggage being loaded. You know, we're the only airline that handles baggage by tossing them underhanded.

Travis (giggling): Did I tell you that one of the passengers fell out of his seat! We hit turbulence and he couldn't keep his stance. Surfers!

Karen: It's a good thing we haven't had a passenger get a thingy caught in the zipper because that would be a lawsuit worth millions...and if the media trivializes things we could end up looking like MacDonald's.

(Karen's voice trails off as she sees the pilot and co-pilot enter the cockpit. She purposely averts the pilot's gaze).

Travis: But you know who really makes out like bandit don't you!

Karen: (Blushes slightly) No. Who?

(Camera focuses on Karen's inquisitive face then fades out for a commercial break).

SCENE 2:

(Passengers begin boarding the aircraft. Travis and Karen are at the front of the plane greeting passengers. Two male German passengers take their respective seats in First Class).

Passenger 1: Eeed-yot! These seat belts are for skinny people!

Passenger 2: And dainty fingers—not sausage fingers like ours.

Passenger 1: That steward who greeted us, could he not make it as a pilot? (They laugh).

Passenger 2: He must have Attentive Deficit Disorder! I've had my light on for nearly five minutes. What lousy first class service!

(More robust laughter).

SCENE 3:

(The Captain and Co-pilot are having a friendly chat before starting on their checklist).

Captain: You know, we ought to serve the passengers beef jerky. We'd save over 10,000 pounds on our weight & balance calculation and increase our ground speed by 30% not to mention saving the airlines millions in food costs.

Co-pilot: That's a great idea! And the airlines could make a fortune on beverages from thirsty passengers.

Captain: I think I'll mention it during my evaluation next week. The suggestion might increase my raise. My wife Shirley has a healthy spending habit when I'm out of town.

Co-pilot: (Shyly changes the subject) Can I take the aircraft off this time?

Captain: (Smiles) Sure! Just ease her off the runway this time. Don't yank back so hard. We've got some elderly folks on board.

Co-pilot: (Eagerly) Yes Sir!

SCENE 4:

(Karen and Travis are in the aft section of the aircraft having a break during the in-flight movie)

Karen: Passenger in row 7, seat 7B wanted my phone number. I gave him the registration number off the Airworthiness Certificate. Sometimes this job gets to me especially for the amount of pay we're getting risking our lives and putting up with passengers.

Travis: (Fanning himself with the flight safety laminated chart) Well, if anyone has it made, it's the pilot's wife. She has hubbie's bank account to squander and no hubbie most of the time so lots of freedom to do whatever with whomever.

TO BE CONTINUED IN THE NEXT EPISODE!
NOT REALLY.

0-595-30586-5

LaVergne, TN USA
10 December 2009

166630LV00009B/164/A